Tom Neely

Tom Neely

Tom Neely

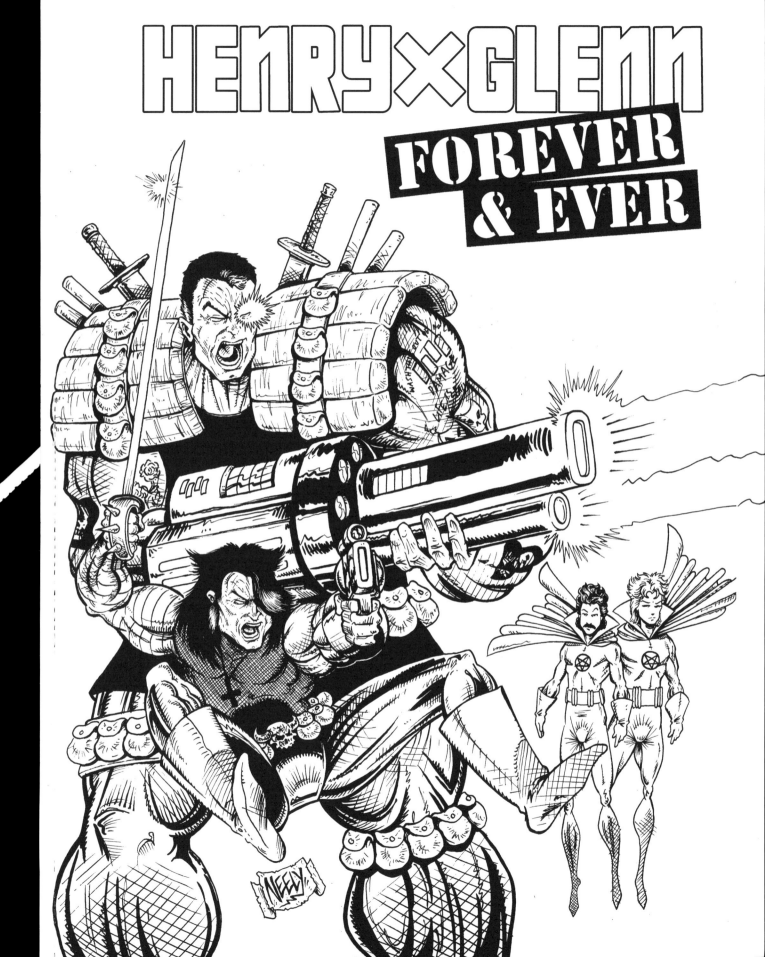

Tom Neely

Tom Neely

Tom Neely

Shaky Kane

Rafer Roberts

Tom Neely

Don Pablo Pedro

Carmen Monoxide

Beth Dean

Rachel Adler

Ed Luce

THE BLACK SPERM OF MY VENGEANCE

Ed Luce

Coop

Tim Sievert

Alex Delaney

Matt Crabe

Katie Skelly

Willow Dawson

Keenan Marshall Keller

Jim Rugg

Tom Scioli

Tom Neely

For this page: BLACK CRAYONS ONLY!!!

Tom Neely

Tom Neely

WHEN YOU ONLY SEE ONE SET OF FOOTPRINTS, I WAS CARRYING YOU.

Tom Neely

LET'S TRY SOME ACTIVITIES!

HOW TO DRAW GLENN!
THE EASY WAY!

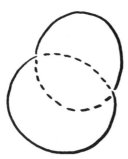

1. START WITH TWO OVALS LAYING OVER EACH OTHER.

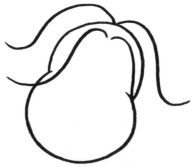

2. NEXT BEGIN THE HAIR WITH SOME "S" SHAPED LINES. LIKE A SEAGULL SITTING ON HIS HEAD.

3. ADD THREE TRIANGULAR TIPS TO FINISH HIS BANGS AND MANE.

4. ADD THREE MORE TIPS BEHIND HIS CHEEK AND THEN FILL IT ALL IN WITH BLACK!

5. DRAW A SIDEWAYS "C" FOR A NOSE, AND A "O" FOR HIS EYE. (NOTE-HIS OTHER EYE IS ALWAYS BEHIND HIS HAIR.)

6. LET'S GIVE HIM A HAPPY LIL' SMILE AND WE'RE DONE!

Practice drawing Glenn on the folowing pages!

Keep practicing!!!

Keep practicing!!!

Use this page to draw SATAN!

HOW TO DRAW HENRY
THE HARD WAY!

1. START WITH A BROKEN SQUARE BECAUSE I'M DAMAGED!

2. GIMME GIMME AN EAR SO I CAN HEAR, AND A NECK TO BANG MY HEAD!

3. STRONG BROW AND A CROOKED NOSE TO MAKE ME LOOK TOUGH!

4. MY EYES LOOK LIKE ARROWS. MY EYES WILL PIERCE YR SOUL!

4. I MAY BE SMILING BUT IT ONLY HIDES MY SEETHING RAGE!

5. DON'T FORGET MY HAIR! I'M NOT A FUCKING SKINHEAD!

Don't be WEAK! Go practice some more!!!

Keep practicing!!!

Use this page to draw some KITTIES!

Can you draw the many MOODS of Glenn?

Happy

Sad

ANGRY!

ANGRIER!

Sad again

Lonely

Tom Neely

Can you draw the many MOODS of Henry?

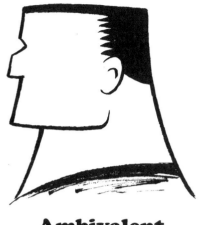

Ambivalent

Tempered

Agitated

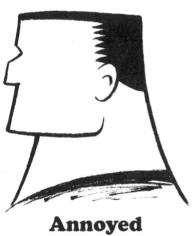

Annoyed

Bottling it all in...

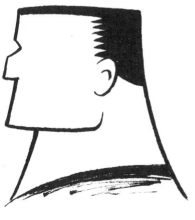

HULKING OUT!!!

Tom Neely

Ed Luce

HENRY

TYPECAST FILM ROLE HENRY
"SURVIVALIST/NEO NAZI"

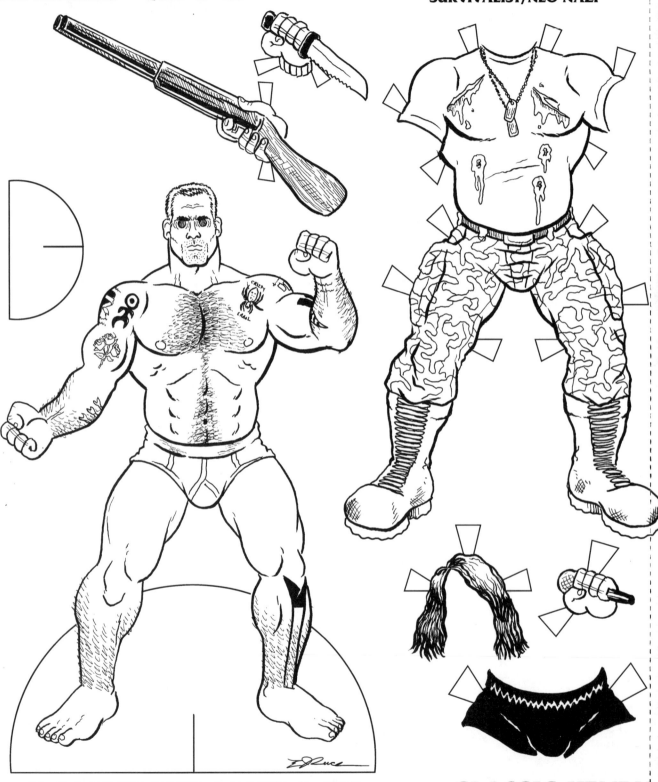

GREATEST HITS PAPER DOLL
by ED LUCE

CLASSIC HENRY

MARRIAGE EQUALITY
HENRY

GAY RIGHTS
ACTIVIST HENRY

SUPERLIAR
HENRY

INTELLECTUAL
HENRY

DAMAGED
THE CAT

Ed Luce

Ed Luce

BEACH GLENN

SABAOTH THE CAT

MARRIAGE EQUALITY GLENN

DANZIGERINE

CLASSIC GLENN

GLENN

CLASSIC SOLO GLENN

GREATEST HITS PAPER DOLL
BY ED LUCE

Ed Luce

Scot Nobles

Fill in the book titles on Glenn's bookshelves!

Scot Nobles

Scot Nobles

Q F R S I R A G E M O W R C A O K D I E N
Y I M A L I A R H R W T V P A R T Y N O P
F H G T P S U D E V I L S P L A Y T H I N G
J A L G D E T S N S A T A N D H R F V A T
I T E E N A G E R F R O M M A R S A H K E
G E N R Y B B O Y J H O G I M M E T O W F
U P N E D O O N G O A T E S A G I M M E G
L U J W A N Y L H E L L U R G I M M E R W
P I O R M E S Y H A L L O W E E N O O E H
D H D Y A B S N U M B E W F D C U T O W Y
E N E I G O K I T T I E S D U O A K H H O C
X W R O E O U O H D H I J D N T D E W L S
H K P P D T L F R E S H S T E P R R H F A
T O N A T Y L Y H M L I A R G H F C O K Z
M H B X W H O O O O A H Y E A H V A A G X
N A H Q O S W O O N B C X W R P A T H V X

CONNECT THE DOTS.

PRAY TO SATAN.

Scot Nobles

Ed Luce

Ed Luce

Kristina Collantes

Kristina Collantes

Kristina Collantes

Mark Rudolph

Mark Rudolph

Tom Neely

THANKS TO J. BENNETT AND DECIBEL

Tom Neely